Paul the Doll

ISBN 979-8-88685-534-0 (paperback)
ISBN 979-8-88685-536-4 (digital)

Christian Faith Publishing
832 Park Avenue
Meadville, PA 16335
www.christianfaithpublishing.com

A special thank you to Mathew Howard for his help with editing.

Printed in the United States of America

Paul the Doll

Tracy Frielinghausen

Ages seven and up

One spring day, a girl named Melissa sat outside with a group of children. A young teacher with short black hair full of blue highlights was telling them all a story. With wide eyes, the children listened to every word the woman said.

The story talked about God. Melissa didn't know what the word *God* meant. She thought, *I don't understand.* But she was a curious child and wanted to know more. She paid close attention.

At the end of the story, the teacher closed the book. She asked, "Do you have any questions?"

Melissa raised her hand. When the teacher called on her, she asked, "Is God real?"

The teacher said, "Yes."

Melissa had more questions. "What does it mean to pray?"

The teacher said, "Prayer is when you ask God for something."

Melissa wondered to herself, *Then all I need to do is ask. Will God will come to me?*

She heard a voice that said, "Yes."

Excited, Melissa leaped to her feet. "Can I leave, please? I need to go home right away to pray!"

Off she ran without waiting for an answer.

Melissa took a deep breath outside her home. Then she opened the door. She found her favorite doll, the one she called Paul. Paul was broken. Melissa picked him up. She closed her eyes and asked God to fix him.

Her dad heard her. He walked into her room and asked, "What's wrong, little one?"

Melissa cried and held up her doll. "He's broken! But today, I learned I can pray, and God will come to me. I'm waiting for God to fix Paul."

Dad picked her up. "God works with all of us and through us. I can fix Paul. I know how."

Melissa gave Paul to her dad. She said, "You can? Why did I ask God when you knew how to fix Paul all along?"

Dad said, "I didn't know Paul was broken until now. You asked God to fix him, and here I am."

Melissa said, "I think I understand. My teacher said God is as all things and all love. Can I pray for anything? I pray for good grades!" She laughed.

Dad set her down. "Yes, but you still need to work for good grades. God will lead you on how to earn them. Be aware of how God answers your prayers. Prayers only work when you have love in your heart. You had love for Paul while praying for him, and your prayer was answered."

Melissa said, "I love you, Dad!"

He said, "I love you, too. Now let's give Paul the love he needs to get better."

About the Author

Tracy Moreland Frielinghausen, a woman who wanted to write a book about her health struggles, is determined to be free of pain.

Now she writes how her awareness of God helped her find solutions and cures that were causing pain and inflammation. She learned through positive affirmations and prayer to trust her instincts and use her imagination to bring the outcome she desired. She shares her experience in the best way she could think of—write children's books.